Who Was
Henry VIII?

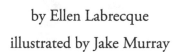

by Ellen Labrecque

illustrated by Jake Murray

Penguin Workshop

For Joseph and James Gallagher—EL

For Mom and Dad—JM

PENGUIN WORKSHOP
An Imprint of Penguin Random House LLC, New York

Text copyright © 2018 by Ellen Labrecque.
Illustrations copyright © 2018 by Penguin Random House LLC. All rights reserved.
Published by Penguin Workshop, an imprint of Penguin Random House LLC, New York.
PENGUIN and PENGUIN WORKSHOP are trademarks of Penguin Books Ltd.
WHO HQ & Design is a registered trademark of Penguin Random House LLC.
Printed in the USA.

Visit us online at www.penguinrandomhouse.com.

Library of Congress Control Number: 2017047153

ISBN 9780448488547   10 9 8 7 6 5 4

Contents

Who Was Henry VIII?

Henry VIII, the King of England, sat at the head of the long table. A trumpet blast alerted the hundreds of guests that dinner was about to begin. The tables were covered in fancy tablecloths and scattered with flowers and herbs. Before the meal began, a priest said the blessing.

Then, servers carried dish after dish from the kitchen. The plates were filled with roast pig, pigeon, peacock, and deer.

On an average day, Henry and his guests could eat six oxen, forty sheep, twelve pigs, and 240 pigeons! Loaves of bread, dishes of butter, and leather jugs filled with beer were set on the table. A fountain spouted gallons of wine for the guests to enjoy.

When the dinner was over, sweet tarts made with fruits from the royal garden were served. Henry ate the most and laughed the loudest of all. At the end of the banquet, he was given a gold cup filled with sweet wine and served wafer cookies stamped with the royal coat of arms. It was just a typical dinner for the king, but it was also quite a performance!

Henry VIII was the all-powerful King of England from 1509 to 1547. He liked to do everything in a big way, especially eating, drinking, and throwing parties. He was very rich and spent a sum equal to $6 million a year just on parties and celebrations!

But Henry could also be selfish and sometimes cruel. He was impulsive and lost his temper quickly. To anger the king in the 1500s was to risk your life. He had tens of thousands of his subjects put to death, including many brilliant men, simply because they disagreed with him.

Henry VIII grew to believe that only God could tell him what to do. What this really meant was that he didn't listen to anyone but himself. Throughout his reign, Henry did anything he wished—for the good and the bad—of his country and people.

CHAPTER 1
Young Henry

Henry VIII was born Henry Tudor on June 28, 1491, in Greenwich Palace in London, England. His parents were King Henry VII and Elizabeth of York.

The Tudors were a very religious Catholic family. The leaders of England had been Catholic for over a thousand years. They followed the teachings of the Pope in Rome, who is the head of the Catholic Church. Therefore, their subjects did, too. England was a Catholic country.

Henry VII had become king in 1485, after thirty years of civil war known as the Wars of the Roses.

Henry VII and
Elizabeth of York

The Wars of the Roses (1455–1485)

The Wars of the Roses was a long series of violent battles in England between families in the cities of York and Lancaster. They fought over who should rule the kingdom. The York family's symbol was a white rose, and the Lancaster family's was a red one. Both families had claims to the throne because they descended from the sons of Edward III, who ruled England from 1327 to 1377.

The Wars of the Roses finally ended on August 22, 1485. Henry VII, the head of the Lancasters, defeated and killed Richard III, head of the Yorks, in the Battle of Bosworth Field.

After his victory, Henry VII married Elizabeth of York, Richard's niece. Through his marriage, Henry VII wanted to unite the two families. His new dynasty was called the House of Tudor.

Baby Henry was born a prince into a rich and royal world, but he was not born to be king. When Henry arrived, he had an older brother, Arthur, age four, and an older sister, Margaret, nearly two. Arthur, as the king's eldest son, was the heir to the throne.

During Henry's early years, a staff of servants took care of him. This was common practice with royal people at this time. The servants did everything for him, including feeding, changing, and bathing him. Two official "rockers" rocked Henry to sleep every night.

When Henry was four, his parents had another daughter, Mary. Henry spent his time in the royal nursery with his sisters and the servants who took care of his every need. Henry's older brother, Arthur, lived in his own private home, where he was being prepared to become the next king. As the only boy in the nursery, Henry was spoiled.

Henry was a good-looking boy with red hair. He dressed in the fancy clothes of the time, including green velvet gowns lined with fur, high leather boots, and caps with ostrich feathers on top.

Henry loved to play outside. He enjoyed tennis, horseback riding, archery, and hunting. He was a gifted athlete and could ride a horse at an early age.

Because he was a rich prince and had the best tutors, Henry read a lot and he was very bright. He was taught by some of the smartest people in England! One tutor called Henry a "brilliant pupil." He studied astronomy, science, and math. Henry also had a passion for religion and maps. Many fancy maps hung throughout the palace. And Henry never got tired of looking at them.

Henry learned to speak many languages, including French, English, Latin, and Italian. He never minded studying, because he loved to read. He even filled up his books with handwritten notes in the margins.

Henry also loved music. He had a good singing voice, and also played the lute—an instrument like a small round-backed guitar. A group of musicians followed him wherever he went. They called him "the harmonious prince."

Outside of Henry's royal world, life was hard for common people during this time. Servants did everything for Henry. But average people did everything themselves. They had to get their own water from wells, make their own clothes, and grow or catch their own food. Most children never even went to school to learn to read and write.

Henry's life was exceptional. As a member of the royal family, he was a very special young boy.

CHAPTER 2
Heir to the Throne

In 1501, when Henry was ten, his fifteen-year-old brother, Arthur, married Catherine of Aragon of Spain. Catherine was sixteen. She was the daughter of King Ferdinand II and Queen Isabella I, the rulers of Spain. Spain was the most powerful country in Europe at the time. The marriage united these two royal families and established an important alliance between their countries. It was intended that when Henry VII died, Arthur and Catherine would become the new King and Queen of England.

Catherine of Aragon

King Ferdinand II (1452–1516)
and Queen Isabella I (1451–1504)

When Ferdinand II of Aragon and Isabella I of Castile married in 1469, their union formed the kingdom of Spain.

Ferdinand and Isabella were both Catholic. As rulers of Spain, they forced everyone in their country to practice Catholicism. People who practiced other religions, such as Judaism or Islam, could either convert, leave Spain, or be killed.

Ferdinand and Isabella also supported explorer Christopher Columbus on his voyage across the Atlantic Ocean. They paid for Columbus's ships, as well as his crew. They also gave him the money and supplies he needed for his journey. When Columbus arrived in America in 1492, he claimed the New World for Spain.

Arthur and Catherine were married for less than six months when Arthur became sick and died. Suddenly, Henry was next in line to be King of England! But he was only ten years old. Henry's father wanted to save England's alliance with Spain. So he promised King Ferdinand II that Henry would marry Catherine, once he was old enough. While Catherine—who was six years older—waited for Henry to grow up, she lived in a palace in London.

On February 11, 1503, Henry's mother died after giving birth. The king had lost his queen and his oldest son in the same year. His surviving children were Margaret, Mary, and Henry. Henry's father became overly protective of his only remaining son. The king forced Henry to spend his time studying safely in a room next to his own bedroom.

Henry wasn't allowed to leave the palace unless it was through a private door into a park. And when he did leave, somebody had to accompany him at all times.

Henry did not complain about being so closely watched. He understood he was next in line to rule England. He had to be protected.

When Henry was seventeen years old, his father grew sick. On April 21, 1509, King Henry VII died at the age of fifty-two. Just two months later, Henry would be crowned king.

CHAPTER 3
Happy Henry

Young Henry was now a handsome young man. He was over six feet tall, and strong and muscular. The typical man at this time was only five feet four inches.

"When he moves, the ground shakes under him," a visitor said about Henry.

He also had a beautiful head of reddish-gold hair.

On June 11, 1509, Henry married Catherine. Many people in England didn't approve of this marriage. Catherine—at age twenty-three—was older than the typical bride in the sixteenth century. Some people feared she was too old to have children. Others thought it wasn't right for a widow to marry her dead husband's brother. But Henry didn't care. He told his advisers that

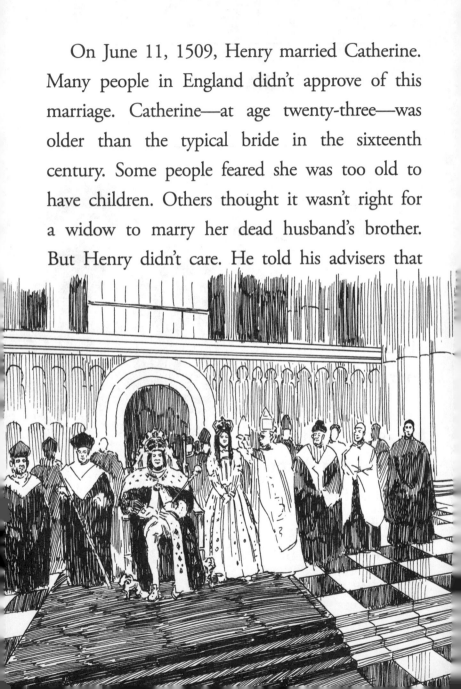

"he desired her above all women," and he loved her.

Just two weeks after his wedding, on June 24, Henry was officially crowned King of England.

A party was thrown in the new king's honor. Henry wore a kingly red robe made of velvet that had fur and rubies stitched to it.

He and his new queen watched jousting matches from a small castle built just for this occasion.

Jousting

Jousting was a sixteenth-century tournament sport. Men on horses charged each other, trying to knock their opponents to the ground. The riders held long poles—called *lances*—as they galloped at high speeds toward each other. The two competitors dressed in suits of armor and held shields to protect themselves. The winner was the man who remained on his horse at the end of the joust. Jousting was popular with knights, nobility, and people of the royal court.

Henry's father had not been a popular king. People thought he was greedy. They thought he imposed high taxes on his people so he could have more riches for himself. In contrast, young Henry was upbeat and bighearted. His subjects loved him right away. He allowed poor people to visit the castle. He listened to their stories of hardships—such as not having enough money to take care of their family.

Often, Henry agreed to help them. A person close to Henry said, "The king has a way of making every man feel that he is enjoying his special favor."

One of Henry's first acts as king was to free prisoners who had been thrown in jail unjustly. Then he had his father's two favorite tax collectors killed for taking so much money from the people. The English people celebrated in the streets of London.

CHAPTER 4
Life at Court

As king, Henry lived in many different palaces. He owned more houses and castles than any English ruler before him. He spent most of his time in Greenwich Palace in London, where he was born.

Greenwich Palace

But he had two other palaces in London: Whitehall Palace and Hampton Court Palace. And he sometimes traveled to Windsor Castle in Berkshire, among others. Henry moved around a lot so his palaces could be cleaned while he was away.

When Henry moved, his entire court went with him. Henry's royal court included servants, such as cooks and gardeners, his friends, wealthy noblemen, artists, writers, and any other people Henry appointed. His court was made up of over a thousand people! Many people wanted to be close to Henry.

As king, Henry gave the orders and commands. But he relied on his Privy Council to do the actual day-to-day work for him. The Privy Council was a group of about seventy men, including lawyers, priests, and aristocrats, all chosen by the king. They gave the king advice and helped him set policies for England. The council met often, but Henry rarely attended the meetings. He simply couldn't be bothered.

Henry also worked with Parliament, the English government. Although he rarely met with them, either, members of Parliament and the Privy Council both understood: No final decision was ever made without Henry's approval.

Parliament

Parliament is the elected body of the English government. It is made up of the House of Commons (elected members) and the House of Lords (originally made up of bishops and noblemen). Parliament's job is to make new laws for the country, to set taxes, and to oversee the government. During Henry's time, Parliament only met occasionally, leaving much of the day-to-day operations of the country to the Privy Council.

The Houses of Parliament

When Henry wasn't busy making important decisions for the country, his daily life was spent eating, reading, hunting, and hosting parties at his different palaces and castles. The kitchen typically served dinner to six hundred people each day! Henry also just enjoyed relaxing and talking with Catherine. At night, they would often go on top of the palace roof to gaze at the stars.

Henry had inherited a fortune from his father—about $478 million in today's money—and could spend it any way he chose.

In addition to parties and food, Henry spent his money on the finest clothes made of silk and velvet for himself and his queen. He also loved jewelry.

A member of his court wrote that, "His fingers were one mass of jeweled rings and around his neck he wore a gold collar from which hung a diamond as big as a walnut."

He also paid sixty musicians to play at his court. Henry loved music. He made sure it was played at all times: at ceremonies, mealtimes, and even when he entered or exited a room.

Even Henry's favorite pets enjoyed the king's wealth. The royal dogs wore silk coats and collars made of velvet, gold, and pearls.

Henry also spent a lot of money on books that he had sent from France and Italy. In the 1500s, the Renaissance movement was just emerging in England. Henry believed deeply in the importance of learning. After all, he was a very well-educated man.

The Renaissance (14th–17th Centuries)

The Renaissance (the French word for *rebirth*) began in Italy in the 1300s but spread to England and other parts of Europe by the 1500s. The Renaissance marked a period of new learning in many areas including art, literature, science, religion, and politics. Two of the most famous artists of this time were Leonardo da Vinci and Michelangelo. The period also marked a time of discovery and exploration of new land, including the Americas.

The Renaissance was made possible by the invention of the printing press in the mid-1400s. Before the printing press, books had to be copied by hand and were only available to the wealthy people who could afford them. They were rare, so education was quite limited.

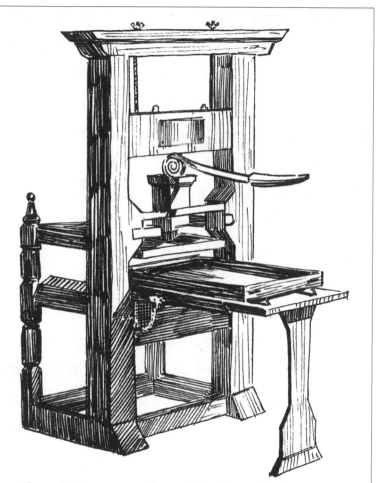

The printing press allowed books and other written material to be mass-produced. This meant ideas could be shared and spread more rapidly.

Henry's court was filled with smart men who could speak and write about many subjects, including science, literature, and religion. It was said that, "[Henry's] court abounds with greater numbers of the learned than any university." The most famous was Sir Thomas More, a statesman, scholar, and devoted Catholic. Henry often invited Sir Thomas into his private rooms to talk about astronomy, geometry, and world affairs.

Catherine was also well-educated. Like Henry, she enjoyed having such smart people at court. But her most important role was to give birth to a son. Henry's number-one desire from the time he became king was to have a male heir so that his family would continue to rule England. Henry was determined to keep the political power in his family, the Tudor dynasty.

Heir to the Throne

Although there was no actual law in England forbidding a woman to rule the country, when Henry came into power, a daughter of the king had never done it before. Traditionally, the firstborn son—and only the son—became the heir to the throne. If a king had no male heir—only daughters or no children at all—fights and even wars could break out to decide who would take control of the country and become the next King of England. Because of this, every king wanted and needed a son to carry on his family's reign.

On January 1, 1511, Catherine gave birth to a baby boy they named Henry. The people of England celebrated the king's son. Shouts of "Long live Catherine and the noble Henry!" and "Long live the prince!" were heard all over the country. And Henry—who was obsessed with having a son—probably celebrated the most.

But the celebration was short-lived. Nearly two months later, the newborn prince suddenly died. Henry was heartbroken. He had already lost his mother, his father, and his brother. And now his firstborn son had died. He needed something to distract him from this great loss.

CHAPTER 5
Off to War

Henry had always wanted to be a great warrior. He held fighting tournaments regularly at his palaces. Men wearing metal helmets and breastplates fought with swords and bows and arrows. Henry often joined in on the fighting, too. One of Henry's men said of the king at this time, "There are many young men who excel in this kind of warfare, but . . . the most interested in the combats is the king himself . . ."

Henry wanted to show his subjects he could fight as well in battle as he did in the tournaments. Another person in his court described Henry "as eager for war as a lion."

England's biggest enemy was the country of France, situated just twenty miles away, across the English Channel.

The two countries had fought over land for centuries. Henry decided to try and conquer France once and for all. He and  Catherine's father, King Ferdinand II of Spain, worked together to invade France. Henry asked his chief adviser, Cardinal Thomas Wolsey, to lead this battle. Cardinal Wolsey was a high-ranking priest of the Roman Catholic Church and Henry's closest friend at court. Henry always valued Wolsey's advice.

In June 1512, an army of fifteen thousand English troops was supposed to join Spanish troops and attack France from the southwest. Henry stayed

Cardinal Wolsey

home, but he inspected the troops before they sailed for Spain. "Never had a finer army been seen," he boasted.

But King Ferdinand II never sent Henry's army on the mission it had arrived to do. He really just wanted the English troops to act as a shield while his army attacked Navarre—an independent nation between Spain and France. He left Henry's troops and moved northward without them. The English army was left stranded in Spain, without

France

Spain

Navarre

enough supplies to survive. They did not have enough food, drink, or even tents. The food they did have made them sick. Many English soldiers died. After four months in Spain, the surviving soldiers came home without anything to show for their trip.

But Henry was eager to prove himself in battle. He did not give up. He and Wolsey decided to attack France on their own. Henry would actually lead the battle this time. After a year of preparation, his army crossed the English Channel and invaded northwest France.

In the Battle of Spurs, the French were taken by surprise. Because they weren't prepared to fight, they fled in panic. All that could be seen of them as they rode away was the spurs on their boots. England easily captured the French town of Thérouanne (say: ta-roo-AN).

Before he had left for France, Henry had set up troops to defend northern England. He was afraid his neighbor Scotland would take advantage of his time away and attack England.

The United Kingdom

Today, England and Scotland are part of an island nation called the United Kingdom (UK). The UK consists of England, Scotland, and Wales (which make up the island of Great Britain) and Northern Ireland.

But during Henry VIII's time, Scotland and England were bitter enemies. Scotland fought many wars to remain an independent nation. But in 1707, Scotland officially became a part of the United Kingdom when they joined England to form Great Britain.

Catherine was in charge of motivating the northern defense troops. And Scotland did attack, in September 1513. But the English troops did their job. Catherine's father had let Henry down, but Catherine did not. "Your grace shall see how I can keep my promise [to protect England]," she wrote to Henry in a letter.

After the battles were over, Henry took credit for both victories. He held a party in London, with a huge feast, dancing, and a play, in celebration. The court poet wrote many poems filled with only praise and love for Henry.

CHAPTER 6
London Riots

In February 1516, Catherine had a healthy baby girl who they named Mary. Henry was disappointed his new child wasn't a boy. But he tried to hide his disappointment and called his new baby his "pearl of the world."

Henry was now dealing with problems in his own country. Riots erupted in London in May 1517.

Merchants from Italy and France had come to London to sell and trade their goods and had ended up staying. The English people did not like that foreigners were living in "their" city. The English rioters destroyed the French and Italian merchants' homes. Henry, just shy of his twenty-sixth birthday, was frustrated. He did not like the damage and chaos the riots had caused. He wanted peace and order on his streets.

Henry had more than four hundred English prisoners from the riots captured and declared them all guilty of *treason*—betraying their own country. Many of them were eventually pardoned and set free.

But thirteen of them were hanged. Their bodies were displayed all over London. Henry wanted to show his own people what happened if they disobeyed him.

Violent and public punishments like this one were common during this time. King Henry VIII and other rulers before him thought this was necessary to make sure their subjects obeyed the law. The public displays of punishment were also a kind of entertainment. English citizens were curious to see people hanged and even tortured. Sometimes the heads of criminals were displayed on spikes at the top of London Bridge as a warning. His loyal subjects did not want to upset the king!

London Bridge

Completed in the early thirteenth century as England's first stone arch bridge, London Bridge spans the river Thames in the center of London. The bridge was the only road across the river in London until Westminster Bridge opened in 1750. Rows of shops lined the bridge's roadway, and houses were built on top of the shops.

In 1831, a new London Bridge was built and the original was torn down. The second bridge lasted until 1968, when it, too, was dismantled. The current London Bridge, built between 1968 and 1972, is the one that stands today.

The violent
riot outbreaks
by his countrymen
were not Henry's only
frustration. His wife,
Catherine, had not yet had
a son. Henry began to wonder
why she could not bear a healthy
son. He feared God was punishing
him because he had married his
brother's wife. And even though he was
married to the queen, Henry had many girlfriends.

This made Catherine especially unhappy. She
was afraid that one of Henry's girlfriends would
have a son before she did. But Catherine was the
queen. She knew that the next ruler of England
should rightfully be her and Henry's child. But
Henry was so obsessed with having a male heir.
He began thinking about leaving Catherine, who
was now thirty-two, to marry another woman.

CHAPTER 7
The Great Matter

Henry and Catherine, like most of the people in England at this time, were Catholic. The Catholic Church, led by the Pope in Rome, forbid divorce. It was against the Church's teachings. In a Catholic country like England, the king was the leader of the country, but the Pope held enormous power as the head of the church. So even though the king did mostly as he pleased, the Pope and his priests had influence over people and nations. Henry's friend Cardinal Wolsey personally asked Pope Clement VII to make

Pope Clement VII

an exception for Henry and allow him to divorce Catherine. But the Pope would not budge.

Henry was furious at the Pope, and also mad at Wolsey. He believed that if Catherine could not have a son, he should be free to marry someone else. He accused Wolsey of treason—betraying his country—and had him arrested. Wolsey died in November 1530, on his way to trial.

Henry decided to ask Parliament to grant him a new title that would be even more important than the Pope.

The members of Parliament feared their king. They served Henry, not the Pope. They knew the king could have them all killed if he wanted to. So the members of Parliament voted to give Henry the new title of "supreme head" of the Church of England in 1531. This required English citizens, who were Catholic, to break away from the Pope's teachings, too. Henry was now in charge of England as well as his new church: the Church of England.

Around this same time, other European countries were rebelling against the Catholic Church, too. But they were opposed to the Church for different reasons than Henry's selfish desire for a divorce.

Martin Luther (1483–1546) and the Reformation

Martin Luther

Martin Luther was a German monk who felt that the Catholic Church had become too rich and too powerful. On October 31, 1517, Luther posted a list on the church door at Wittenberg University, where he taught religion. The list contained ninety-five different items he was rejecting about the Catholic Church, including how the Pope accepted money and favors in return for forgiving people's sins.

Luther thought people's faith in God should be more personal and private, without the Pope or priests being involved. Luther's protest grew into a movement called the Reformation. By 1529, the movement had spread across Western Europe into England. Luther's followers began calling themselves Lutheran Protestants because they protested the rules of the Catholic Church. There are over eight hundred million Protestants in the world today.

Anne Boleyn

Henry didn't really care about Martin Luther or the Reformation. He just wanted a divorce. He had fallen in love with a woman named Anne Boleyn. Anne worked as a lady-in-waiting for Queen Catherine. A *lady-in-waiting* is a trusted friend and companion to the queen and princesses.

Henry wanted Anne to be his girlfriend. But she refused. Anne wanted to be his queen, not just his girlfriend.

Now that Henry was the head of his own church, Parliament granted his divorce from Catherine. And on January 25, 1533, Henry married Anne Boleyn. Catherine was no longer queen. She was sent off to live in a cold, damp castle for the rest of her life. Their daughter, Mary, now seventeen, lived about nine miles from Henry in a different palace. Although she was well cared for by servants, Mary was not allowed to see her mother. Henry feared that his daughter and his first wife might make plans against him.

CHAPTER 8
Off with Her Head!

Queen Anne gave birth on September 7, 1533. But to Henry's disappointment, it was another girl. They named her Elizabeth.

As Henry became more desperate to have a son, he grew even more selfish and ruthless. Henry worried that many English people might turn against him because they didn't approve of his separation from the Catholic Church.

He also knew that they weren't happy about his divorce from Catherine. She had always been a popular queen, especially since she helped stop the Scottish invasions years earlier. Henry feared the English people might rise up against him.

In 1534, he forced Parliament to pass a law that said only his and Anne Boleyn's children could inherit the throne. He also made Parliament declare it against the law to say anything bad about the king! If a person was caught, they were accused of treason—a crime that was punishable by death. It was the job of Thomas Cromwell— Henry's new chief adviser—to make sure these laws were obeyed.

Thomas Cromwell

Cromwell hired people to snoop for him. People caught speaking out against the king were killed.

One man who didn't agree with the new laws was Sir Thomas More, Henry's former good friend and adviser. Even though he knew he faced death, Sir Thomas wanted to remain Catholic and follow the Pope's teachings, not Henry's. Because of his defiance, Sir Thomas was beheaded on July 6, 1535. Before his death, he claimed he died "the king's good servant, but God's first." Henry could easily get rid of anyone who didn't agree with him, but it brought him no peace.

In January 1536, Henry was thrown from his horse in a jousting accident at a tournament at Greenwich Palace. He hit his head hard against the ground and his horse fell on top of him. Henry was unconscious for over two hours. Members of his court thought he was going to die.

Henry did recover, but he wasn't the same man after the accident. He was forty-four years old. He constantly suffered from very bad headaches. And an earlier wound on his leg had become infected. It made walking painful for him. Perhaps because he was in constant pain, Henry seemed upset and angry much of the time. He became quite cruel. And the jousting accident may have injured his brain more than anyone realized.

Henry went from being a once generous and jolly king to becoming a mean and selfish ruler. He still did not have a son, and so he started to worry. Henry wondered if he would ever have an heir to rule the kingdom in his place. And he began eating more and more.

At this time, the common person ate mostly vegetables and bread, a few times each day. Henry ate more than *thirteen* times a day! He feasted on chicken, beef, rabbit, and swan. He grew quite fat. And he was very unhealthy.

In this state, Henry quickly became tired of his new queen. He had married Anne, but Henry still had many girlfriends. Anne was not happy about it. And she told Henry so. Henry expected his wife to obey him, not to argue with him.

Henry didn't bother to ask his wife for a divorce this time. He decided to treat Anne like any other British subject who had broken the law. She had said something bad about the king, so he had her put to death. On May 19, 1536, Anne was beheaded by order of the king.

Just eleven days after Anne was killed, Henry married twenty-seven-year-old Jane Seymour, who was a member of the official court. Jane was much more shy than Anne and did not argue with the king.

Jane Seymour

CHAPTER 9
Oh Boy!

Even though Jane was now queen, Henry could not give her a proper *coronation*, or celebration, in her honor. After decades of spending money on his homes, clothing, jewels, paintings, books, and parties, the royal treasury was empty. Henry and Thomas Cromwell came up with a plan to become rich again.

In an act called the Dissolution of the Monasteries, Henry's soldiers and officials looted Catholic convents, cathedrals, and monasteries all over England. Because Henry was no longer Catholic, he considered these church-owned properties to be his. They were filled with holy relics, gold, silver, and valuable objects. Devoted Catholics had visited them over the years and left behind a lot of money and jewels in prayer and thanks.

The monasteries also maintained valuable farmland. Over four years, Henry seized property and treasures worth millions of dollars. Henry also demanded that more than five hundred Catholic churches be locked or torn down.

Lost Treasure

During the Dissolution of the Monasteries (1536–1540), Henry VIII destroyed and stole wagonloads of valuable and important jewels. One of the most well-known gems was a huge ruby donated by Louis VII, who ruled France from 1137 to 1180. The ruby had been set in the gravestone of Thomas Becket—an English religious leader in the 1100s who was also considered a Catholic saint. Henry took the ruby for himself and had it turned into a thumb ring.

Nobody knows for certain what happened to this valuable ruby, but there is a rumor that Henry VIII was buried with it.

Wealthy once again, Henry began to make peace with his two daughters. Mary, the daughter of Catherine of Aragon, was now twenty. Elizabeth, daughter of Anne Boleyn, was only three. Mary had sided with her mother over the divorce and Henry had kept her living apart from him for years. Catherine had died earlier that year. But his new wife encouraged Henry to forgive Mary. Henry relented. Mary was invited back to Hampton Court Palace and Greenwich Palace. Henry largely ignored young Elizabeth, but she lived comfortably under his servants' care. Mary, however, often visited with her half sister.

Unfortunately, Henry wasn't at peace with his subjects. After he looted the church properties,

the English people began to
complain about their king. Henry was rich once
again, but their taxes remained high. There were
also some English citizens who still considered
themselves Catholics and had never joined the
Church of England.

They soon decided they had had enough. They were going to rebel against the king. Thousands of armed men protested in the north. Henry was afraid they would march to London. The royal army wasn't big enough to fight them. Henry wanted to stall the rebellion. He sent one of his men to talk to the rebels for him. He promised to lower taxes and stop stealing from the monasteries. The English rebels believed him and returned home.

But Henry had lied. And he ordered the rebel leaders to be killed. As a warning to his people to never again turn against him, Henry hung their bodies from trees all over northern England.

CHAPTER 10
A Bitter and Sad Ending

While Henry was busy suppressing the rebellion, he soon had good news. Jane Seymour finally gave birth to a son. Edward was born on October 12, 1537. Henry wept for joy. But his happiness was brief. Just days after Jane gave birth to Edward, she died from an infection.

Henry mourned the death of his wife. But he finally had the son he so desperately wanted. That was enough for now.

Since Henry finally had his heir, he became obsessed with keeping his son healthy and protected. This was just how his father had treated him when he was young. Henry feared Edward would die from an illness or that an enemy might try to kill him. Edward lived in a heavily guarded section of Hampton Court.

Hampton Court Palace

Hampton Court Palace in London is one of only two of Henry VIII's palaces that still stands today. (The other is Windsor Castle.) During the second half of Henry's rule, he spent more time at Hampton Court than any other palace. His son, Edward, had been born there, and his third wife, Jane, died there.

During Henry's time, he built a great hall, as well as royal tennis courts, at Hampton Court Palace. The hall alone took over five years to build.

The royal family has not lived in Hampton Court since the eighteenth century. It is now open to the public for tours.

Visitors to Hampton Court were allowed near young Edward only if they had a handwritten order from Henry himself. Nurses and nannies had to wash thoroughly before touching the prince. Henry did not want his son to become sick. He was not taking any chances.

Even though he worked very hard to keep Edward healthy, Henry wasn't satisfied with just one son. After all, Henry's older brother, Arthur, had died before he became king. Henry wanted insurance—a spare heir—in case anything happened to his first son.

Henry married for the fourth time on January 6, 1540, to Anne of Cleves. Anne's brother, William, Duke of Cleves, was the leader of a Protestant German state. Under the advice of Thomas Cromwell, the marriage was arranged to help England form better ties to other countries in Europe.

But Henry, who now weighed over three hundred pounds, soon decided that Anne wasn't pretty enough! He ended the marriage just a few months later.

Henry blamed Cromwell for encouraging him to marry a woman he didn't think was good enough for him. Cromwell had helped Henry get his first divorce. And in return, Henry was now accusing Cromwell of treason. Henry had him executed on July 28, 1540.

In all of England, no one else could declare an end to a marriage, or end someone's life for such ridiculous reasons. Henry was now doing whatever he wanted, whenever he wanted. The British government had given him this absolute power, and he used it freely.

Catherine Howard

Henry married Catherine Howard on the same day Cromwell was executed. Catherine was just sixteen years old—thirty-three years younger than Henry. She had been a lady-in-waiting to Anne of Cleves, so she had known Henry from the royal court. But it was becoming dangerous to marry this King of England. And it certainly was dangerous to marry the king and send love letters to another man. But that is exactly what Catherine did. Henry discovered her letters and had her beheaded in the Tower of London in February 1542.

Henry's sixth and final marriage was to Catherine Parr, the daughter of an official in the royal court. Catherine was more of a nurse for Henry than a wife. Years of excessive eating and drinking had made the king very fat. He was fifty-two years old and he weighed over 350 pounds. He had difficulty walking.

Catherine Parr

Servants carried him from room to room in a chair covered in gold velvet and silk. Extra supports had to be put in his bed frame so it didn't collapse. Henry still went hunting, but he could only shoot while sitting on a raised platform.

Henry was running the country about as poorly as he was living his personal life. He yelled and screamed a lot. One of his first biographers described Henry during this time as "the most dangerous and cruel man in the world." If he didn't like somebody, Henry would have him killed. Nobody was safe from Henry's temper. It is estimated that Henry had more than seventy thousand people executed during his lifetime. It is hard to imagine just how angry a man Henry had become. He was growing older, becoming even more unhealthy, and he was afraid of losing control of his kingdom.

In the last couple of months of his life, Henry barely got out of bed. But his servants never talked to him about death. They feared his anger and knew it was considered treason to predict when a king was going to die.

One of Henry's servants did ask the king if he wanted to speak to any "learned man." It was custom at this time for people on their deathbed to confess their sins to a priest, who were some of the most educated men of their day. Henry responded, "I will first take a little sleep, and then, as I feel myself, I will advise upon the matter."

These were the last words Henry VIII spoke.

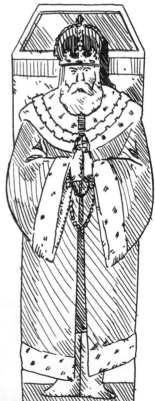

On January 28, 1547, he died at the age of fifty-five. Henry's body was put into a coffin, but he was too heavy. The coffin burst open from the weight of his body and had to be repaired. When it was fixed, it was covered in cloth spun of gold. A wax sculpture of Henry was placed on top of the coffin, as was done for all important people at the time.

The statue of Henry had a crown of precious stones on its head and jeweled bracelets and rings on its hands. Henry's body was placed to rest in a tomb in a chapel graveyard outside of Windsor Castle.

Henry's son, Edward VI, became the new King of England. He was only nine years old. Because of Edward's young age, *regents*—or advisers in the government—ruled the country. Edward died at the age of fifteen, just six years later, on July 6, 1553. The country was divided between Catholics and Protestants. Henry had wanted to be a good king who united all of England. That task would now fall to someone else.

CHAPTER 11
Larger Than Life

Henry lived his entire life wishing for a son who could inherit the throne when he died. He couldn't imagine a way for his family to continue ruling without a prince who would one day become king. Living without an heir nearly ruined Henry's life. But interestingly enough, without a surviving male heir, his two daughters stepped in.

Henry's first daughter, Mary I, became the first queen regnant of England. That means she was the first woman to serve as queen who had absolute power to rule. Mary ruled as a Catholic and had many Protestants put to death. But she was queen for only five years. After Mary's death, Henry's second daughter, Elizabeth I, became the Protestant ruler who saved the Tudor dynasty.

Mary I

Elizabeth I (1533–1603)

Elizabeth I was the daughter of Henry VIII and Anne Boleyn, Henry's second wife. A governess, tutors, and servants raised Elizabeth in the country, away from London. When she was twenty-five, in 1558, Elizabeth became Queen of England. At the time, the country was broke. It was also divided between Catholics and Protestants.

Elizabeth was a brave and smart woman. During her reign, she defended her throne against Spain and France and made England a strong and rich country once again. When she died in 1603 at the age of sixty-nine, England was one of the world's greatest powers. Henry, who thought a woman could never rule England, would have been shocked by how great a queen his daughter had become.

Today, nearly five hundred years after his death, Henry VIII's larger-than-life reputation lives on. Countless television shows, movies, books, and plays are still written and performed about him and his excessive lifestyle. One of William Shakespeare's most well-known plays is called *Henry VIII*.

And even the current Queen of England, Elizabeth II, is related to Henry! She is a member of the family of Henry's older sister, Margaret, the grandmother of Mary Stuart, Queen of Scots.

During his lifetime, Henry went from being a beloved ruler to a spoiled and feared king who no one dared question. He wasted the goodwill that he had created among his subjects by becoming obsessed with his own legacy and his desire to have a son. But in the end, it was his daughters who helped preserve his family name by becoming the very first two Queens of England.

It was said that Henry "was undoubtedly the rarest man that lived in his time." After all these centuries, this is still true today: Henry VIII will forever be remembered as a king like no other.

Timeline of Henry VIII's Life

1491	Born June 28 in Greenwich, England
1502	On April 2, Henry's older brother, Arthur, dies
	Henry becomes heir to the throne of England
1509	On April 21, King Henry VII dies
	Henry VIII is now the King of England
	Marries Catherine of Aragon on June 11
1516	Mary Tudor is born on February 18
1527	Asks the Pope to grant him a divorce from Catherine
1531	Declares himself supreme head of the Church of England
1533	Marries Anne Boleyn on January 25
	Henry and Anne's daughter, Elizabeth, born on September 7
1534	The Act of Supremacy "officially" confirms King Henry as the supreme head of the Church of England
1536	Anne Boleyn is beheaded on May 19
	Henry marries Jane Seymour on May 30
1537	Edward VI is born to Jane and Henry on October 12
	Jane dies twelve days later
1540	Marries Anne of Cleves on January 6
	Marries Catherine Howard on July 28
1543	Marries sixth wife, Catherine Parr, on July 12
1547	Dies on January 28

Timeline of the World

1492 — Christopher Columbus takes his first voyage across the Atlantic Ocean

1503 — Leonardo da Vinci begins to paint the *Mona Lisa*

1517 — Martin Luther starts the Reformation in Germany

1519 — The Spanish Conquest of the Americas begins

1520 — Ferdinand Magellan reaches the Pacific Ocean

1526 — The printing press is introduced in Stockholm, Sweden

1532 — *The Prince* by Niccolò Machiavelli is published

1534 — Reformation begins in England

— Sir Thomas More is executed

1543 — Nicolaus Copernicus publishes his theory that the sun is the center of the solar system and the Earth and other planets revolve around it

1546 — Martin Luther dies

1547 — Ivan IV, or Ivan the Terrible, is crowned czar of Russia

Bibliography

*Books for young readers

Ackroyd, Peter. *Tudors: The History of England from Henry VIII to Elizabeth I*. New York: Thomas Dunne Books, 2012.

*Dwyer, Frank. *Henry VIII*. New York: Chelsea House Publishers, 1988.

*Green, Robert. *King Henry VIII*. New York: Franklin Watts, 1998.

Hutchinson, Robert. *Young Henry: The Rise of Henry VIII*. London: Weidenfeld & Nicolson, 2011.

Starkey, David. *The Reign of Henry VIII: Personalities and Politics*. New York: Franklin Watts, 1986.

Weir, Alison. *Henry VIII: The King and His Court*. New York: Ballantine Books, 2008.

Weir, Alison. *The Six Wives of Henry VIII*. New York: Grove Press, 1991.